Information Technology Defense Contracting

So you want to be a contractor?

Gustavo Coutin II

authorHOUSE®

AuthorHouse™
1663 Liberty Drive
Bloomington, IN 47403
www.authorhouse.com
Phone: 1-800-839-8640

First published by AuthorHouse 05/21/2011

ISBN: 978-1-4567-6249-0 (e)
ISBN: 978-1-4567-6248-3 (sc)

Library of Congress Number: 2011907409

Printed in the United States of America

Acknowledgements

My wife and daughter deserve most of my gratitude for being there when I come home from my globe-trotting and for being there when I need a sympathetic ear or guidance on one of my many missions.

I am grateful to my parents for their inspiration, especially my mother. She was living proof that intelligence comes in many forms. May she rest in peace.

Finally, I am grateful to all of the family members and people who were blurs on the high speed road of my life. May we all get a chance to see each other more often than in the past. But please know that I acknowledge you as an important part of my journey.

Dear Reader,

Let me guess. You're reading this book because you are looking for new opportunities to use your skills and be paid in a satisfactory way. You want to use your time for all it's worth to buy that house, pay down that mortgage, finance your kids' education, drum down that debt, and build your savings and investments into a cozy nest egg for you and yours.

You're talented and you want to use your talents optimally. You may have a sense of adventure.

If so, you have come to the right place. This is the guide for you. I want to introduce you to work that has paid great dividends in my own life.

I owe a lot to the world of defense contracting. I was able to pay off $100,000 in credit card debt in one year. Defense contracting has allowed me to support my family in style and afforded me the opportunity to travel and see different parts of the world, all the while knowing I'm serving the causes of our country. It has been win-win all the way for me, and I would like to share these opportunities with you.

I'm talking about contracting with the Department of Defense. You know what they say about the government: They are always hiring! The Department of Defense has over $400 billion dollars in their annual budget for contractors, from food service or road construction to IT work to musicians for marriage seminars! They have jobs abroad and at home. They have jobs in hot zones like Iraq and Afghanistan, and they have jobs in cool zones like Germany, Italy, Greece, Belgium and even thousands of spots right here in the United States.

In general, the rougher the living and working

conditions, the more money you will make. If there is a need for someone to travel to a remote site to work on a system and the only way there is by helicopter or convoy, they are going to pay you more.

The more dangerous the situation, the more money they pay, so it is up to you what kind of risk you want to take on for what period of time. You can make around $300,000 a year in the "hot zones."

Yet there are positions with companies paying $150,000 dollars a year in places like Germany, which includes a housing allowance and a car rental on top of the pay. Who would not jump at an opportunity like that?

The government has jobs. The government has money. You can step up to the plate here and benefit from those two major facts. I am going to tell you how. I wrote this book to benefit you and to benefit the industry that has given so much to me. Read on to learn about bona fide opportunities, real guidance, and solid tips on how to break into the lucrative and rewarding field of contracting for the Department of Defense.

Sincerely,
Gus

Contents

Introduction

Today's economic climate is such that unemployment in the United States is hovering at around 10%. That means on your block or apartment complex, one out of every ten people is unemployed. Recession? They say if your neighbor loses his job, it's a Recession. If you lose yours, it's a Depression. A lot of people are experiencing a Depression right now, and even the pundits call our current economic situation "The Great Recession" and compare it to the Great Depression of the 1930s when ordinary, everyday Americans were standing in bread lines.

Maybe you are lucky and you have not lost your job, or maybe you already have or live with the fear that you will. Maybe you're one of those people whose company has downsized, leaving them in place but asking them to do the work five people used to do while at the same time taking a pay cut. Maybe, even with your job, you just can't get ahead and keep on top of those growing debts.

If you are in any of these situations—or if you just want an exciting new direction in your life—defense contracting may be the answer for you.

A Recession-Resistant Career

What has amazed me is that in spite of this economic climate, defense contracting is a field that is booming. With ever-expanding government, there is so much work, the civilians working in government positions can't do all the work themselves and have to hire companies to assist with the workload. This is where you come in! This is in your interest, and could hopefully lead to the growth of a rewarding career for you.

Contracting is recession resistant. I cannot say it is recession proof as nothing is recession proof, but you could literally leave one job and have another before leaving the airport after your flight out from the old job. With the proper guidance, which I hope to give you, you should be able to set yourself up for success in whatever it is you're trying to achieve.

It is my intention to give you the full skinny on everything you need to know to get into this lucrative and booming field, secure a clearance, and make more money than you ever have doing something I hope you love as much as I do: defense contracting.

Like the branches of the military, the defense industry is always hiring, only they hire people like you and me: civilians or ex-military personnel who are now civilians. They hire us to enable our soldiers and military personnel to do their all-important jobs while civilian contractors take care of the details. In that way, you are contributing to our national interests and causes while furthering you own at the same time. What's not to like about that?

If you have skills they need, it does not matter where you are from. Your social or ethnic background is not an issue, nor is your current income. Develop your skills right, and you can make well over $200,000 a year. This is not an uncommon amount to make for IT experts deployed overseas. There is almost an endless job pool for work both in the U.S. and outside the U.S. while working for U.S. defense industry interests.

This guide will serve as an especially helpful resource for those who work in the field of information technology (IT) for the Department of Defense (DOD) or other agencies for IT is my field of expertise.

Rest assured that the recommendations in this book come from many years of working with different customers and in different environments. Often when a Field Service Representative (FSR) is deployed, that person has the time to really reflect on human nature and the various methods of dealing with individuals on the personal and professional levels. I want to give the wisdom I've gained through my experience to you, so that you can be as successful as I have been in dealing with all the ups and downs of working as a defense contractor.

There is a goldmine of opportunity out there for individuals trying to build their skills and make money. There is a place for you out there too.

Who Do You Want to Be?

Normally, there are two types of contractors: ones who work in the U.S. (CONUS) and those who work overseas (OCONUS). It is my hope and intention to offer a manual for individuals to tap into this almost endless resource, especially in this slow economy with its down-sized job market. The U.S. government assures that a great deal of work is supplied to external, non-government entities. The only real drawback is that the work might not be right in your own neighborhood and you might have to travel at times. For some people, that's part of the attraction: seeing the world through adventures in other lands!

My background consists of many years of military and commercial experience. When I started in contracting I had no degree or any certifications. As I grew in to the field I started working on my Bachelors degree, which I completed, and many industry standard certifications and training. It's hard to believe I am writing a book, but I feel all too often that people don't have the necessary guidance to afford them success in the information technology industry. Most of my experience has been with military systems, so you probably will notice some of the information comes from systems that are already in the works. Though they may appear similar, I assure you that none of the information displayed or discussed is actually an operational network.

Most of the information is drawn from my own personal experiences, and my hope is that it will save at least one field technician a lot of headaches and lost time from lack of knowledge. If just one person can be helped and allowed to grow in the technology field, then the purpose of this book will be achieved.

Is that one person you? I hope so. Read on!

Glossary of Common Terms

ACU	Army Combat Uniform
AOR	Area of Operations, normally a set region that someone works in, for example: The Iraq AOR
CAC	Common Access Card or your ID
CBT	Computer Based Training
Contractor	An individual who works alone or with a company, supporting another company or agency on a temporary, per job basis
CONUS	Continental United States
CRC	CONUS Replacement Center (aka: contractor processing)
DFAC	Dining Facility, chow hall
OCONUS	Outside the Continental United States
FSR	Field Service Representative
PM	Project or Program Manager
PMO	Project Management Office
PX	Post Exchange, shopping area

Resume	A document to assist in getting an individual hired through listing his or her experience and accomplishments
WAR	Weekly Activities Report

Chapter 1: What Is a Contractor?

The most basic definition of a contractor is someone who does work on a limited basis, for a certain amount of time, for a certain fee. A contractor is an individual who works alone or with a company, supporting another company or agency on a temporary, per job basis.

A contract may last a couple of years or months, or it may only last a few days. The contractor may work directly with a company him- or herself, or the contractor may serve as additional personnel for a company that is itself contracting with the larger entity, this is called sub contracting. Contracting is different from full-time employment and very different from full time enlistment in the armed services.

Many businesses in the United States are turning to contract workers for help in projects rather than taking on full-time employees and having to pay all those benefits and deal with long-term commitments.

The U.S. government was actually the leader in turning to contractors for a lot of their needs. For the armed forces, it meant freeing up enlisted personnel to do military work as opposed to doing all the support work that goes into putting and keeping a modern military force functioning in the field.

If you are a defense contractor, you are someone who works, either through a business or through yourself as an individual, providing services or products to the military. In other words, you may be a contractor or a subcontractor.

In 2007 the U.S. Government spent close to $80 billion in contracts to support their operations, and it has been growing every year since, topping $100 billion dollars per year. Contracting is a growth industry, and government contracting even more so, mostly because the government has a "Use it or lose it" mentality to when it comes to budgeting. If a department is awarded $100,000 to maintain its operations and then they are able to do it for $80,000, most of the time they will spend that extra money on items or services that will better the department, just to assure that there is total expenditure of the $100,000 initially budgeted. Maybe they do this to make sure they get the same budget or a higher one next year. Although we know this may not be the most effective spending of our tax payer dollars, there is always the need to support the government's operations with contracts, which in turn creates a bit of security for the contractor. A contractor can almost always get a new position either within the company he or she is currently working with or else with one of the thousands of other contracting companies that work in the defense industry.

In the contracting world, contractors are the crème de le crème of their field. They are the people you call when your equipment or your people aren't working right; they are people you call when you have a need to be filled or a problem to be solved. A contractor adds validity to a contract and calmness to chaos by bringing in his or her wisdom and logic to whatever system requires it.

Normally, a company will hire a person as a contractor

to support another contract or operation that they have been hired to support by the primary employer (such as the DOD). So say company ABC has a contract with the government, but they need additional support to grow a new contract in Afghanistan. ABC hires company DEF and contracts them to add the additional personnel and to assure the growth and expansion to accommodate a surging requirement in the field, this is how the sub contracting process works and allows for a bit of spreading the talent across a few companies instead of just one.

A defense contractor is called a field service representative (FSR for short) because he or she is in the field, working with the customer, getting hands on with whatever work he or she was hired to assist with. The FSR is chosen because he or she is the number one expert in the contracting company, or because of the fact that no one else wants to go (which is often the case with government contract work and working overseas, especially in "hot zones") and he or she is going there to alleviate some situation or problem.

If you are an FSR, you might not know everything, but you should have the resources and the contacts to arrive at a solution for whatever the problem is.

As an FSR, you might show up for just a few days to work out a particular problem, or you might be the kind who is assigned for many weeks or months. There are even those that are embedded with military or government units to offer advice and solutions to missions for years at a time. This last one is the one that this guide is mostly aimed at, but it does not preclude any of the others.

Long term contractors may find that there is a difference between what is being done and what needs to be done, and part of the job may be getting everything on track—in a personable way, of course, which I will go into in Chapter 5. Chapter 5 will cover customer service, but for now let me say that usually the best attitude to have is that you are there to support your customer in any way you can (and maybe for as long as is needed).

Most of the time a contractor will have a set mission or parameter to a mission known as the "statement of work" that outlines your tasks and time frame. It is a good idea to read a copy of this, normally provided by the company trying to hire you, so that you can be aware of the operation you are hiring into. The job could be to support a Promina on a network that contains many other pieces of equipment, or to support the complete logistical warehouse that a military unit is operating in its AOR (Area of Operations) or it could be something entirely different.

You don't necessarily have to get in with a big firm to become a government contractor. The government encourages small businesses too, and has allotted lots of money to them, especially women-owned businesses, minority-owned businesses, and veteran-owned businesses. You can work for a small business rather than a giant corporation and get plenty of contract work.

No matter who you work with, the government is definitely open for business!

Chapter 2: What Do Contractors Do?

All sorts of skills are needed by the U.S. government and the Department of Defense. One recent DOD listing called for piano and guitar players to create a beautiful and unique atmosphere at some marriage-strengthening seminars they were holding for army personnel and their wives at Fort Dix, New Jersey! No matter what your talents, you can be of service and get paid well for it too.

Some of your first steps as a contractor are to define what services and/or products you have to offer. Since my experience is primarily as an IT contractor, let me explain what an IT contractor does and how I arrived in the wonderful field of Defense Contracting. I have usually worked as a subcontractor with companies who themselves have contracts with the DoD.

My career started on a large project in Kosovo in 1999. This was my first time traveling and entering the contracting arena and I have to say it was one of the most inspirational experiences I have ever had. The friendships I formed during this period carry on even today. The work allowed me to see and experience a country that I would never have left home to see if it were not for contracting. To see the Serbians and Albanians up close and learn their culture after seeing only the war from the TV in my living room in the U.S., was absolutely amazing.

During my twelve-plus years in this industry, I have seen a lot of the world. I've been to some countries I had never even heard of before, such as Djibouti and Kyrgyzstan.

Most of my time has been spent in the Middle East, and I have been privileged to see Jordan, Dubai, Kuwait, Bahrain, Saudi Arabia, and Iraq to name a few. This does not even include the European countries, such as the Netherlands, Germany, Italy, and Spain. What great times you can have being able to travel and work doing something you love with someone else paying the bill!

In Country or On the Job

Once you are in a country as an IT contractor, it will often be a typical assignment for you to work new systems into the old or "legacy" equipment. That is one of the most common assignments. Your customer should set you up with all the players on the system to allow you to get the answers that you need, and normally they will introduce you to the people you will be working with. This allows for ease of your integration into the troubleshooting procedure.

Trust me when I tell you this is not often the case and your presence can lead to some egos being hurt or a bit of attitude towards you as the technician and the new kid on the block who is there to "fix" their problems. I'll give you more tips on how to integrate with the existing team in Chapter 5 on Customer Service, and I'll give you a few tips later on in this chapter as well, as integrating into the team and the procedures is crucial to your success as a contractor.

If at all possible, research the old and the new systems to have a better understanding on how they work and how the customer has them integrated into their current enterprise. Find out everything you can.

The usual order events to a contractor arriving on site should be similar to below:

1. Introductions are made to the people in charge. This allows you to know who your direct point of contact is. If at all possible, establish this well in advance of arriving on site. At least try to have a list of names and positions so you know who is who.

2. Have the management explain to you what it is that they are trying to accomplish and what their end goal is.

3. Meet the other players on the system, including administrative staff and technicians.

4. Take some time to figure out what the people on the ground think can be done and what their recommendations are for the work you're going to do. Make sure you are taking notes on what they say. I will show in a chapter ahead how important documentation is. In addition to that, they will see that you are serious about their input and needs and that you value the information they are able to give you.

5. Explain to all present what you foresee as being the solution to the problem and see if there is proper documentation on the system, such as histories, equipment types, and any notes that might have been kept. If you are able to get these, then you are halfway done with

your job. Fair warning, though: it is rare that documentation is kept.

6. Once you begin work, ensure that you are the one doing the work. You don't want a bunch of hands making changes, no matter how mundane those changes may seem, while you are working on the situation. You must be in control here. Ask people to document any changes they make or want to make and to talk them over with you.

7. Make sure you keep all your own documentation. (More details on this to follow.) This can include notes on the documentation that you were given. This will help in the final write up on what needs to be done to get to where the customer wants to be.

8. When you believe that you have corrected the problem or decided on what solution to apply, consult management and let them know what it's going to take. You also might want a person from the technical team to be present so that you don't have to repeat yourself.

9. Finally, write up everything that was done and also everything that is going to be done as you see it and submit this through email or directly to the decision maker.

Now this might not always be the exact configuration of steps that will be taken with and by the customer, but it should serve as a general guide to getting established with the customer and getting to work with the least amount of ego clashing. Though normally a contractor is brought in to assure that a system is up to speed and maintained, as I indicated earlier, a contractor can easily be seen as the guy who is going to make someone feel demeaned because you are coming to work on their system, which clearly needs help. Assure the people around you that you're there to assist them in getting to a resolution, not to make them look bad.

Remember to learn about and from your environment first. There is no need to be overly anxious or boisterous when you're working on a new project. Sit back, relax, and work your personality naturally into the environment, and your natural skills and personality will eventually just fit. Too often I see technicians come in all loud and noisy because they don't know what they are doing and they lack confidence. Don't be the one to hide your shortcomings by being the loudest in the group. You just may get called out on it. Learn the ropes, learn the systems, and then use your self motivation to go in and learn more than just the basics that will get you to the next paycheck. Don't expect to change the world or learn all about it in a day. Professionalism and skill take time to develop.

CRC: The First Step of Processing

Once you accept a position with a company, there is a process you have to go through to get to where the job is. Part of that process is going through the CRC or CONUS Replacement Center. Here is the official link to Fort Bennings website for CRC:

https://www.benning.army.mil/infantry/197th/CRC/

During your week stay at CRC, you will be housed on base unless your company pays for a car and hotel, which is not uncommon. Housing is in barracks and normally they are either four man rooms or large bays with everyone living together. There is a roll call every morning, and people are accounted for. Though this process is a bit extended and bothersome, it does serve the purpose of assuring you are accounted for in the system and that you have all your shots and medical records done and are ready to go.

Prior to heading to CRC, there should be a bunch of Computer Based Training (CBT) you need to go through, dealing with such topics as counter-terrorism awareness, sexual assault, computer conduct, and many other topics. Have these done prior to getting to CRC, and carry a print-out of your completed certificates, even if your company says you don't have to. The computer could be down, or there could be any number of other issues. If you have copies with you, your processing will proceed without delays. Also, carry copies of your orders. If you have to wait on people to make copies for you, there could be long delays in your in-processing. Make sure you have multiples of all certificates and other relevant papers. It speeds the process up.

Always carry your Immunizations with you for processing and while at your final work destination. There are some countries, especially in Africa, that will require proof of certain shots and immunizations. I suggest carrying your shot record with your passport. That way it will not get lost.

Note the acronyms that may be used in your in-processing. These are found at the beginning of the book. Some of them will be new to you if you have not worked with the Defense of Department before.

Once you start processing, along with an average of 300 other people, you will be in a lot of extended lines, and there will be a lot waiting time. I recommend that you bring a book or small computer to make the time pass a bit better. This is a primary example of the saying "Hurry up and wait." The people working at the CRC have done this process numerous times and basically have it down to about as good a science as they possibly can, but it still takes time.

If your company tells you to take something to CRC, make sure you have it prior to your arrival. Normally such things as medical records, birth certificate, and the like are the normal types of documents called for.

The process will be run according to which branch of the military you will be working for. For Marine contractors, you will in-process at Camp Leugune, which has smaller groups and tends to be a lot faster. The link for this CRC is:

http://www.marines.mil/unit/mcieast/dpc/Pages/DoD-Civilians-Contractors.aspx

The Marine CRC tends to be a bit more combat-oriented. You will go through the tear gas chamber. If you have never been in the military, this may be exciting and will offer you many stories to tell. For those of you who are vets, this process will be really tedious.

Remember that the process has been in place for quite some time and you whining or sighing heavily about how slow and unorganized the system is will not speed it up any. Bring your book and relax. Go where you are told to go. The personnel there are doing things the way they were told to and probably don't have much say in making any changes.

I have been to CRCs at Fort Bliss, Fort Benning, and Camp Lejeune; each has their good and bad aspects. I like the Marines CRC, as the groups are smaller, and you are in and out quickly. The whole process will still take about a week, no matter where you go. I recommend that you arrive early and be where you are supposed to be when you are supposed to be there. If you are on time, you are already late.

Chapter 3: Who's the Boss?

If you are a contractor, who is your boss? The government? The military? The company you contract with? I recommend that you work with a company that does defense department contracting, for reasons I will go into, and obviously, that company is above you. Still, in many ways, you are your own boss when you are a contractor.

Within the contracting realm there is a chain of command. There is your company's chain of command, then there is the project oversight chain of command that could include your company and the customer's representatives, and finally, there is the customer's chain of command. These positions are as varied as the positions you are filling. I will attempt to break it down for you, but this is by no means the *de facto* way that it is arranged.

This description from Wikipedia explains quite a bit:

"Unless specifically prohibited by another provision of law, an agency's authority to contract is vested in the agency head, for example, the Secretary of the Air Force or the Administrator, National Aeronautics and Space Administration. Agency heads delegate their authority to Contracting Officers, who either hold their authority by virtue of their position or must be appointed in accordance with procedures set forth in the Federal Acquisition Regulation. Only Contracting Officers may sign Government contracts on behalf of the government. A Contracting Officer has only the authority delegated pursuant to law and agency procedures. This authority is set forth in the Contracting Officer's certificate of appointment (formerly called a "warrant"). Unlike in commercial contracting, there is no doctrine of apparent authority applicable to the Government. Any action taken by a Contracting Officer that exceeds the Contracting Officer's actual delegated authority is not binding on the Government, even if both the Contracting Officer and the contractor desire the action and the action benefits the Government. The contractor is presumed to know the scope of the Contracting Officer's authority and cannot rely on any action of Contracting Officers when it exceeds their authority. Contracting Officers are assisted in their duties by Contracting Officer Representatives (CORs) and Contracting Officer Technical Representatives (COTRs), who usually do not have the authority of a Contracting Officer." (See: http://en.wikipedia.org/wiki/Government_contract#The_Contracting_Officer).

The Contracting Officer is a key person for you to know about. This person has a lot of authority delegated to him or her by the government or branch of service.

However, I recommend you work with a company that contracts with the government rather than dealing directly with the government yourself. This helps you in a number of ways that are well worth it, such as having all your support and services paid for instead of you having to worry about all the logistics and support that are involved with supporting the contract.

The way it works is this: the government may put a posting out there for a networking engineer to work with the military. The company you are signed up with then is paid a certain amount of money, let's say $100 dollars an hour for the position. They then turn around and post a position for a Telecommunications Technician at $35 dollars an hour with full benefits and a minimum of ten hours a day. They throw in hazard pay, differentials, and bonuses. With that whole package, you have a pretty good job offer. Now you understand how the company makes money off you, but don't forget that they also assure you lots of little perks, like training, extra days off, benefits, and other options that may be important to you. Normally these costs are able to be claimed back to the contract, so the company loses nothing, or at worse claims the usages on their taxes.

Defense contractors are in defense contracting to make money; the more money they make with the least effort the better their financial outcome. There is a lot of overhead in larger companies that eat into their profits: such things as HR representatives, payroll people, and managers who all take money away from the total that your position is making for them. Normally, contracting companies spread this expense out across many departments or contracts. That is the genius of this operation: they take a cost from one contract or department and spread it out so that profits are shown. With this good performance, the contracting company then approaches another contract with the ability to say that their costs were kept down and they have had a great performance review on past contracts. This is how companies keep people employed. The better they are at managing the money, the better off you are in your position and future with that company.

One last note on who's the boss: You may be given some sort of fancy title for your contract job. That's nice. Let me assure you, though, having an impressive title is not as important as making sure you get the money and benefits you want. If you're called a janitor and you're working on a large enterprise network making $200,000 dollars, so be it. Be the best network janitor you can be, and don't worry about the title. The goal is to achieve the end results you want, like paying off debt, as I did, or paying off that house, or sending your kids to good schools and universities. In that way, let me tell you, as long as you are working toward and achieving your personal financial goals, you are the real boss.

A contractor is always in the process of getting his or her next job, because a contractor is, in many ways, an independent business person, even if he or she works for a contracting company. That's one reason why I say you really are your own boss in this business. Some good contractor job hunting tips are the subject of the next chapter.

Chapter 4: Job Hunting Essentials and the Resume

There are many ways to get the jobs that you want or need to sustain you. One way is to post on some of the more modern websites for job placement. Word of mouth or subcontracting are other ways to go about it. Depending on your experience and how targeted you are in your job hunting, I recommend online websites.

The one I use all the time and exclusively for DoD work is www.militaryhire.com. I found that they are the best to target my job search in the DoD arena, and I can narrow down the search to areas and keywords. It is best to pick one or maybe two websites and stick with them. Otherwise, you will tend to get way too many pieces of junk mail, and a lot of times the keywords you choose will get you even more useless hits.

When job hunting, remember that you must be able to get the work that you want by targeting the specific field that interests you. If you want to work in computer programming, then you need to target that type of company and do web searches for your career prospects. It would not behoove you to go to mixers with nothing but information analysts milling about if you are trying to get some of the jobs dealing with computer programming. Although having contacts in different industries can be useful, you just won't get the immediate return on your job search efforts that you would with targeted meetings.

Always carry a copy of your resume with you, either on a mini disk or a memory stick. I like to put mine on a memory stick and a phone; that way I will always have one or the other with me, just in case there is a need to pass out my resume to people. Your resume should be in a chronological format and should cover all your relevant years of experience.

It does not matter in the world of contracting if your resume is four pages long or not. People are going to want to see if you are a fit for their particular position. There will be times that you will not be a good fit in an organization that you may be currently working in. A good fit is important. Yet even if you find yourself in a work situation where you are not a good fit, before making any hasty decisions, make sure that you have something else lined up for your next career move.

The resume is your first contact with a company, or at least its first legal contact with you. There has to be an understanding between the hirer and you that your resume is for a position and that position is the only position that should be used with your resume, unless you give express permission to use it for other positions. I mention this because when you give someone your resume, and that company or individual is using that resume to secure work, your resume might be used to say: "This is the type of people we hire." You don't want that. You don't want it being used for any other means than what is beneficial to you. After all, you put in the time and effort to build the skills to get you where you are today, and that effort should be utilized for your benefit and the benefit of the company that hires you to do their work.

I recommend the following format for your resume. This format has worked well for me, and with today's OCR (Optical Character Reader) you want to ensure that all the keywords are in your resume in the right way of presentation. The best approach is to not bunch up all your keywords in one section, but to spread them out across the resume to cover all relevant information.

Below is a sample resume format with notes embedded. Just remove the sample wording and plug in your own information.

JOHN SMITH

555 Nowhere street • Sunny, Florida 12345 • 555-555-5555 •
John.Smith@Name.com

(Note: Here you want to put positions that you would like to be in line for, this could be positions other then the one you are applying for)

(Example:) **IT Management • Director • Senior Manager • Technology Management • Information Security Current Active Top Secret Clearance**

PROFILE

Brief description, no more than four paragraphs explaining your whole working career in a relevant manner that is short and to the point. This part is to sum up why you would be an asset to the company you are applying to.

(Note: Here you want to put your general abilities that could apply to you working with the company)

(Example:) **IT Operations • Program/Project Management • Strategic Planning • Team Building •**

PROFESSIONAL EXPERIENCE

(Note: only list the last ten years of relevant experience in this section)

Company name, company location   Years worked
Job Title

Here you just need a couple of sentences about the type of work that you performed. This should be relevant and to the point. This is not the place to list all the equipment and type of work that you did.

- Then short, bulleted, explanations of work done.
- Such as: Maintained $1M in equipment inventory with zero discrepancies

Company name, company location   Years worked
Job Title

Here you just need a couple of sentences about the type of work that you performed. This should be relevant and to the point. This is not the place to list all the equipment and type of work that you did.

- Then short, bulleted, explanations of work done.
- Such as: Maintained $1M in equipment inventory with zero discrepancies

Company name, company location   Years worked
Job Title

Here you just need a couple of sentences about the type of work that you performed. This should be relevant and to the point. This is not the place to list all the equipment and type of work that you did.

- Then short, bulleted, explanations of work done.
- Such as: Maintained $1M in equipment inventory with zero discrepancies

Company name, company location   Years worked
Job Title

Here you just need a couple of sentences about the type of work that you performed. This should be relevant and to the point. This is not the place to list all the equipment and type of work that you did.

- Then short, bulleted, explanations of work done.
- Such as: Maintained $1M in equipment inventory with zero discrepancies

(Note: Always put your name centered at the top of each page, in case the pages get separated)

ADDITIONAL EXPERIENCE

(Note: This is for experience more than ten years back)

Company Name
Years worked
Job Title (Location worked)

Company Name
Years worked
Job Title (Location worked)
Company Name
Years worked
Job Title (Location worked)

EDUCATION

(Note: This is for your formal education, such as a college or university)

Degree attained or working towards, college or university name

CERTIFICATIONS & TRAINING

(Note: Possible breakdown of your training and certifications)

- Management: Comptia Project +, ITIL v3.0 Foundation Certified
- Cisco:
- Security:
- Microsoft:
- Other Certifications:

TECHNICAL SKILLS

(Note: here is where you list your individual products or equipment that you have worked with)

(Example:) **Windows, Linux, UNIX, MS Office, Project, Visio, Acrobat, Photoshop, FrontPage, Active Directory**

I recommend that you use Times New Roman as your font. The reason for this is that OCR (Optical Character Readers) has an easier time to pick up keywords in this format. No matter what format you end up using for your online resume, remember you want to have the keywords towards the top. This way the hiring manager knows right off the bat if you're a fit for the position.

Another situation to be wary of is when hiring managers try to hire you to fill any old position and not a position that is suited to your skill set. You will waste many years and a lot of time working in positions that may not interest you or are not a fit for you at all. Remember, you are in charge of your own destiny, and to assure your job satisfaction, make sure you take a job that will be a fit and still challenge and prepare you for the next level in your career.

Career Titles

There are a number of ways that companies handle job titles. They may use them for pay scales or for showing seniority on a project. One of the standards that should be adhered to is the roles and responsibilities that come with a title. For instance, below are the job descriptions for a Network Engineer career track:

Network Administrator: Handles inputs that are directed from above. May handle many inputs into similar or dissimilar devices, such as switches and routers. Does what is directed with minimal decision making.

Network Technician: Handles the same duties as the Network Administrator and also decides which is the best way to get the end result directed by engineering or management. This may include deciding on the breakdown of IPs for router or switch and assuring that all systems operate as advertised, such as RF distances and proper cabling. Also concerned with cabling and equipment locations.

Network Engineer: Decides the best architecture and layout for the whole network. Guides junior technicians on how to best get the end result engineered. More concerned with the higher view and not really on how the cabling is routed or such things as switch locations.

The reason it is important to know what your actual position's roles and responsibilities are is because that is the basis for your pay. The government could go to company ABC and say, "We need an engineer level network guy," and the company could then post the job as a Telecommunications Technician III. What you, as the job seeker, should be concerned with is the equivalent position that is being billed to the government. This is called a labor category and can be found on the relevant government posting site. For instance, if you are under a General Services Administration contract, you would go to www.gsa.gov and do a search for company ABC's labor costs and codes. Then you would see that company ABC is billing X amount of dollars and paying you Y amount. This will allow you to negotiate your current skill sets to a higher pay scale.

Of course, the company won't tell you this information. This is something that is learned with experience. Once you understand job categories and pay scales, you can hone and direct your skill set attainments toward higher pay.

Equal Opportunity

Equal opportunity employment is a Godsend in the contracting world. Don't hesitate to say your race and veteran preference or sex on any forms. It is important to fill all this out so that you can be assured of any edge it might give you in getting employed. If you are Hispanic, a Desert

Storm Vet, or female, indicate it. Companies sometimes have to hire a certain percentage of women or other groups for their contracts. These are not new rules, and they are not ways of messing up other people's chances. It is just that the U.S. government wants to assure fairness, and they put these rules in place to assure that everyone gets a fair shake, regardless of race, social status, religious beliefs, or other specific factors.

Claim who you are. The government will often reward you for being diverse, and they will award the companies that are diverse also.

Chapter 5: Customer Service and On the Job Tips

I don't exaggerate when I say that whatever your field, but particularly in defense contracting, customer service is what is going to keep you employed. If you plan on working in any field for any length of time, pay attention to this chapter, because it is important to your future.

Remember that your repeat customer is going to quickly become your good buddy. Most work for a company is drummed up among the people who are already working in the field. Repeat customers are people you don't have to sell to again—they already bought, and because you satisfied them, they will return to you again and again.

In any field, all too often, companies suffer because of the poor customer service skills of their employees. An employee of any company needs to be on his or her best behavior and is not allowed an off day when it comes to dealing with customers. When there is an incident with a customer, it does not matter who is at fault. That problem will overshadow all other good dealings with that customer. Is the customer always right? No, of course not, but in the business world the customer is how the company pays its bills and, incidentally, assures you that you have future growth and work with that company.

Customer service is more than keeping the customer happy. It is a whole mindset to do the work in a professional manner and to produce a quality product or perform a quality service. Sometimes this is not achieved due to reasons outside the FSR's control, such as poor management, or the project was not effectively led and constructed. The bad part of this is that you, the man on the ground, are the one who suffers for others' weak work habits.

Remember, though, that if the field tech looks good, then the contracting company looks good; so do your absolute best to provide top notch customer service, no matter what else is going on around or above you. If questions are raised or issues come about, never blow your cool and never let them see you sweat. Appear to be in control, and you will soon assume control of the situation.

Clarifying expectations will help you and your company follow through to the end with a product or service that will cause your customers to want to bring you back on the job again and again. Within this book there will be many different ways guiding you to achieve good customer service. One tip right off the bat is to have the resources available in a handy location so that you can get answers quickly. I will give you more tips to help you learn what to expect and how to plan your work environment accordingly.

Most of the experience that I have gathered over the years has been from both commercial and military contracting, so when I explain customer traits or personalities, I will attempt to let you know what type of customer I am talking about. There tends to be a different mindset when dealing with either commercial or military, so it is imperative that you know your customer. If you are allowed enough lead time, learn as much about your prospective customer as you can. This can be done by doing web searches. Word of mouth often works, but find out as much as you can by whatever means you can (within reason!). By learning as much as you can ahead of time, you will be allowing yourself to get to know your customer better and also how they might react to you and your work.

Social Awareness and that All-Important First Impression

I like to call this social awareness, as you are trying to find out as much as you can about a group or individual for the benefit of that group or individual. (I have written a white paper on this topic. Please see the end of book for details on how to get a copy.) A lot of times people will call this social awareness "social engineering," but there is a difference between the two, which I will not get into at this time. Just be aware that the more you know about who you're working with, the lot better off you will be in the long run. You will be better equipped to cope with any personalities that you might run into.

There are numerous tests out there that psychologists or scientists have devised to break the general populace up into various groups or personalities by either traits or reflections on reactions to a question. As I am sure you are aware, there are a lot more grey areas in a person's personality than are read on the face of our first interactions with someone.

Which leads me into the question: Are first impressions that important? YES, they are very important. If you make a bad first impression, then you will be spending a lot of time recovering from that impression; whereas if you make a good first impression your work will be much more easily accomplished and good rapport will be established and maintained. A book is most certainly judged by its cover. Try dressing up one night and then dressing down the next and watch the difference in people's reactions. Dress shirts and slacks or nice jeans go a long way toward people perceiving the FSR in a positive light. Appearances and visual perception are very important.

Now let's move on to the more internal work: How do you build good rapport with a customer?

Let's look at this by examining two scenarios. In the first, you will create a good impression and be able to integrate well so as to be welcomed into the customer's fold. In the other, you will make the customer and yourself wonder what the heck you are doing there.

In the first, successful scenario, you are introduced as explained in the first chapter. You are meeting with the manager in charge of your project. You opted to wear ironed blue jeans that are in good shape, and you are wearing a nice polo type shirt with brown loafers. The meeting is going well, and then manager decides that he likes you and wants you to meet the rest of the crew or team. At this time you are taken down to meet the people that you will be working closely with, and lo and behold, they are dressed similarly to you. This makes the environment to build relationships in a lot easier. Relationships are half of your job—remember that. You find out that there are a couple people who seem to accept you right into their fold. You will probably gravitate towards them, and this is not a bad thing, but remember this is the first impression, and you've got to keep your options open. Don't limit yourself to one type of personality or group of people (or a clique).

This is how a decent introduction and employment commencement meeting should go, and it means you are on the road to success working with that group of people.

Now let's look at how it could go if you are not informed

about your customer or the people that you will be working with. Not every job will have a polo shirt and jeans mentality, though this tends to be the case in the majority of high tech markets. It's important to know something about your customer on this point, because sometimes it's just as bad to over-dress as it is to under-dress.

Now wouldn't it be nice if all jobs you went to flowed as easily as the one described above? Well, they can if you do your research. Now I am sounding like a broken record, but it is very important to learn about your environment before plunging into it.

In this second scenario, your boss at the contracting company didn't tell you anything about what you would be doing. Basically, he dropped you off and said, "Good luck." You did not have the time to do research, say, due to the fact that this was a rush job that came suddenly and everything happened so fast. Today your attire consists of old sneakers or running shoes, a tee shirt with some obscure band's logo on it, and last but not least your finest pair of worn-out jeans that have been on your body for two days straight.

Now this might be a little out there, but trust me, when it comes to management and prior planning, you hope that your contracting company does their homework and does not just put you out there like bait to be eaten by sharks, like telling you the workplace is extremely casual, for instance.

The big day comes and you show up as described. What do you think will be the outcome of this encounter? First, you are sorely under-dressed. Your appearance already puts you and your customer at a loss. Of course, a bad appearance does not mean that you're any less capable, but the first appearance will leave you way behind in the race to win your customer's hearts and minds. Other important variables will come into play too, like did you show up on time? Do you have an odor to you? Are you wearing cologne? (Normally,

I would recommend not wearing cologne. You never know what others like or don't like, at least not at first, and some may be offended by it.)

Now you're in front of the manager and he's looking at you and the first thing that crosses his mind is: "This kid needs to learn how to dress." The next thing going through his mind is that he will still talk to you, but you're already running up hill as far as initial appearance goes. Still, he talks to you and figures out that you really are the man for the job. Yet if I were a hiring boss, I would not take you to meet the crew on that occasion. I would set another appointment and ask that you wear business casual clothes or something similar. By doing this, he's saving face for both of you. Imagine what his workers would think and say if the manager brought this individual into their fold and he is a misfit from the get go.   When appearing to apply for a position or to meet the customer for the first time, I have to emphasize, do your research and know as well as you can what you need to look like and act like right from the first. Know the job, know the people, and know the environment that you will be working in. Don't allow anything to be a surprise. If something is a surprise, don't let anyone know that it is. Don't let the customer see you sweat. As far as he is concerned, you should appear to know what is going on from the start, and the best way to do that is to do your research, increasing your social awareness.

Working Well with Others

Many times you will have no problem getting the job, but once you're in, you want to stay in, and that's a whole new social and professional skill set. Now you have to work with others, and now you need to show your stuff without inflicting too much damage to anyone's ego or anyone else's sense of belonging or place. So you need to ease your way in, stay quiet, look around your environment, and learn the inner workings of the place and the people. All too often a new FSR will come in, all eager to show what he can do, and in the end all he does is step on people's toes. This might not be what you intended to have happen, but you've got to remember you are just coming in, and there were people there before you. Respect that.

Getting in with the people you work with is pretty much the hard part. You should figure out the boundaries of the environment and the people; for instance one man smokes and another doesn't; one man is a hard worker and another isn't, etc. These nuances are what will make the work an enjoyable experience. That's right: I said enjoyable! Imagine liking where you work and who you work with. What a thought!

One thing that you can do is find out what is the big off duty entertainment that people partake of, like motorcycle riding, game playing or just hanging out at the park. If you can find this out, then you will be involving yourself with the individuals you work with. How often have you had a new guy show up in your work place, and he didn't do anything with the employees, and he pretty much hung out by himself or maybe with a spouse after work? Normally people think that this guy is stuck up or he's not a team player. In actuality this individual might be waiting for someone to approach him, but don't let that individual be you.

I believe the problem is that people all too often feel that they are more important than anyone else in the world. Now I'm not saying that each person or individual is not important, but what I am saying is that people need to sometimes come off that high horse and step in the manure, get down in the trenches, and learn what others are doing and thinking. Allow yourself to see how others see things without being judgmental or analytical about it all.

Leaving

When the work is done and it's time to go home, this is when you need to pay particular attention to customer service. A short timer's attitude upon leaving will kill a nicely built up relationship just as quickly as a bad first interview can. You want to be happy that you did well and that the job is done, but you don't want to act like it was a terrible chore for you to stay and do your job, even if it was. Most of the time people around you might be jealous or mad that you get to "break out" of whatever perceived prison you're working in, so don't fan the fires of that by showing your own relief.

You might have had a really bad time. It happens. For instance, say you take a job overseas with the government, and you had a pretty good time doing your work, but you had no contact with your management, or you found they had a poor reaction time to inquiries, and it just added an air of arrogance to them which led you to believe you weren't important to them and it frustrated a lot of your efforts. Should you show this impression to anyone that you're working with? NO. You do not want your customer to ever know your company's internal weaknesses or deficiencies. Suck it up and either bring it up to your managers or their bosses yourself or look for other opportunities with different contracting companies. Do not let off steam among the customers.

When you leave, leave with a smile and an assurance that you will be back, even if you have no intention of ever showing your face there again. Remember—never burn your bridges if you can help it.

I am sure I am not alone when I say that all too often people don't know what they need to do in order to succeed. It is better to approach troubleshooting and integration of systems with the attitude that you will learn and at the same time grow with the development of your system. Also, you should be aware that all your experience won't matter if you don't have a good relationship with the customer.

I am sure that you are all aware that there is a vast store of knowledge out there, but like a CD with one good song out of twelve, you won't need it all. I want to give you the information you need so that you can carry this book in your success tool kit.

Another part of customer service is that it is imperative that the new and growing technician advance himself and his career by attaining and maintaining various certifications. You have to keep current and even be advancing in order to keep ahead of the game. Whether it is networking, sitcom, or administrative in nature, a person should aspire to achieve more knowledge than just the basics. For instance, if you are working on a satcom system, it would behoove the technician to work on the muxing and crypto side of the house too. This allows even more growth and development of skills, which means you can serve your customers more. There will be more about certifications in the chapter on documentation, but know that the more knowledge you gain, the better you can serve your customers and your own goal of succeeding as a defense contractor.

Chapter 6: A Day in the Life of a Typical IT Contractor

Let me give you an example of how a typical IT contract job goes. Often times the contractor will not be called into fix a problem, but to assist with systems optimization or integration. Normally there are two types of jobs that fall into this category: one is updating older equipment with newer equipment and the other is adding new equipment to an already existing system. Both of these types of work can be very rewarding and offer a lot of opportunity to learn new equipment or procedures. I will say it again: make sure that you keep lots of notes for future reference and career-building potential.

When installing new systems, make sure that you have all the older systems laid out so that you can always return to a known point. This could mean that hard drives are imaged and that you take down all the relevant settings, such as IP addresses and other system configurations and diagrams. If the procedure I'm outlining seems a bit basic, that is done purposefully so that you plan out what you are going to do and you don't just jump into a procedure haphazardly.

Assure that any configurations changes are coordinated with any other personnel, such as a distant end that you are shooting a satellite link to, or you might have crypto or other timing that needs to be matched up. This allows for any discrepancies in timing or such to be handled as they happen and prevents them from becoming a problem down the road. Always do any changes to the system at the least damaging time of the day. Normally this is late at night. This will also allow you to return the system to normal operation if there should be a problem with newly integrated components.

Remember an ounce of planning will allow minimal down time and a more successful upgrade. Why would you work on the kitchen sink if the stove is broken? The ideal situation would be to have redundant systems to test new patches or upgrades to. This is not always possible, but if you are able to get other duplicate components and test on those, it will be an easier sell to the stakeholders as to why you are doing any changes.

I know a lot of this is "Duh" in nature, but trust me when I say that all logic is thrown out the window when dealing with situations that people could lose their jobs over or look bad in. Just take the few extra steps to assure that everything and everyone is in line and onboard.

Assisting with upgrades is a good opportunity to get useful knowledge with a minimal amount of planning from the contractor's perspective. By this I mean that someone else has something in mind that they want to accomplish, and they will be doing most of the planning while you assist. This can be good and bad. It is good in that you might learn something, and bad in that you might pick up some bad habits. Too often people are trying to work within time constraints, either real or made up in their own minds, and also they might be gunning for the boss's approval. This type of individual is the worst type to work with. They tend not to plan well and have really poor working habits. Just because someone works on something for twelve hours straight does not mean they know what they are doing or that any real actual work got done. It is best to be efficient and offer technically sound options instead of just jumping in and spending half your time figuring out what you did and how you did it just to say you worked till 1 a.m. When there is a contractor on site, what takes another person twelve hours should probably take that contractor three hours. Work smart. It will show.

Establish Relevant Contacts

When working in the technical field, it is always imperative to have contacts on various systems or knowledge bases outside of your own. All too often technicians allow their egos to get the best of them and they don't keep others in mind as resources when trying to work through a problem. Exchange business cards and have an open mind that this person could offer you some assistance down the road, or that you could offer him or her some assistance.

It is wise to keep your contacts handy and ask as many questions about a person that you can without being too intrusive. You want to learn as much as you can about this person, if for no other reason than to help you down the road. Remember, you are in the field, and as any one with contracting experience knows, survival is a team effort. Often you will run into people that you met many years ago. One day on a job in some foreign country or city, you might run into someone from the past again. It's always refreshing to see a face you know and especially one that can assist with a problem you might be having working for your current customer. So DO NOT burn bridges if at all possible. Some people are just hard to get along with, but you should attempt to maintain at least minimal working relationships with as many people as possible.

Don't forget that the contact you make today could be the one that gets you a position or some work in the future. Maintain professionalism at all times. Nobody gets along with everybody, and most of the people you work with are never going to be your best buddies. Everyone can end up respecting you, though, and you get that by respecting everyone else.

Do you remember a few year's back, a book came out called *Emotional Intelligence* by Daniel Goleman? That book made the top of the bestseller list. The basic idea was that people who are good at relating to other people, who are good on an emotional level, are the ones who succeed. One of the points Goleman made was that at Bell Labs, they did a study of the star performers. Nobody at Bell labs was bad at his or her job. Most of them excelled, but some people stood out as being exceptionally good at their jobs. They found out through studying them that these star performers had good networks of support through good relationships. When they needed information, they could get it quickly and easily from someone who knew and respected them enough to supply them with the information they needed. That was the only factor that made them stand out from the rest and succeed as much as they did.

Learn to be a good people person, and you will find the resources you need to do an outstanding job and become a contractor who gets called again and again and again. You'll have plenty of "days in the life of" a contractor!

Chapter 7: Certification – The Paper Chase

What makes industry standard certifications such as Comptia, Cisco, and Microsoft so useful in today's technical industries?

This question is often asked of me as I progress through the various certification tracks. For some, the reward is the constant gathering of knowledge and learning of new topics. For others, it is the ability to show documented proof of a skill set.

Often certifications are overlooked or dismissed as the property of a geek trying to show he knows something. This is a false impression. Certification helps an individual develop skills. It shows a company that its staff has the knowledge to complete the job.

A company receives numerous benefits as its staff completes certifications, including credits for education as the staff attends training and certification programs. A good example of the benefits offered to companies using certifications is Cisco, which offers education credits or reduced rates on software and COTS (Common Off the

Shelf) hardware. Both Cisco and Microsoft offer these kinds of perks to a company that uses their certification processes.

These savings not only allow more personnel to be qualified on a process or product, but they also represent a return of investment for the company.

Cisco, in particular, provides a program that recognizes a gold or silver status for a company when a specific number of the company's personnel become certified. A gold status with Cisco allows benefits ranging from free access to portions of the Cisco website to a 30 percent savings on purchases of partner equipment.

Personal benefits enjoyed by the individuals gaining certification include the satisfaction of learning a new skill set and being able to take one's knowledge and apply it to a project. Getting a certificate allows achievable goals and clear reward (certification or passing of a test) for the employee.

When I discuss certifications with others, I like to point out that testing allows me to keep my skills honed and show others that I am ambitious and motivated. It also supports my company with new skill sets and training that are cost effective and relevant to my industry.

My company, Total Technical Solutions, offers classes on Network Plus and Security Plus as well as many others. Check out our website at www.totaltech.us.com for the latest listings as well as the location for the e-book copy of this book.

DOD Directive 8570 and Certifications

The Department of Defense Directive 8570 provides guidance and procedures for the training, certification, and management of all government employees who conduct Information Assurance functions in assigned duty positions. These individuals are required to carry an approved certification for their particular job classification. GIAC and Comptia certifications are among those required for Technical, Management, CND, and IASAE classifications.

The need for these certifications applies to any full- or part-time military service member, contractor, or local national with privileged access to a DoD information system performing information assurance (security) functions, regardless of job or occupational series. The manual, *8570.01M*, specifies that the Department of Defense requires approximately 110,000 identified Information Assurance professionals to be certified within a five year time period. The Defense Information Assurance Program office has divided its Information Assurance workforce into six defined categories. The manual also specifies the types of commercial information assurance credentials that qualify for each of the defined categories.

The list of those who need to be certified is growing every day. Below are the basic requirements of what is needed as of the writing of this book:

• By the end of CY 2010, all personnel performing IAT and IAM functions must be certified.

• By the end of CY 2011 all personnel performing CND-SP and IASAE roles must be certified.

• All IA jobs will be categorized as 'Technical' or 'Management' Level I, II, or III, and to be qualified for those jobs, you must be certified.

I think you get the picture that certifications are just as important as formal education in the modern DoD environment. If you would like more information on the 8570 standard, please check out this link:

www.dtic.mil/whs/directives/corres/pdf/857001m.pdf

What Certifications Should You Get?

I get asked this question a lot, and the short answer is get the certifications that interest you. If you like working on servers, get the Comptia Server plus cert and Microsoft certifications. If you like working on telecommunications equipment, then you could go for industry specific tests such as Avaya, Juniper, and Alcatel. It really depends on how you want to make your money and how you want to make yourself as marketable as possible as quickly as possible.

Obviously for the current DoD requirements, I would recommend the Comptia (http://www.comptia.com) Network Plus and Security Plus tests. These tests are the basic requirements of the DoD 8570.01M requirement, and they are a good base to start to build your IT career off of.

On a last note: "He or she who has the most paper wins." Certification can only help you, as it assures potential customers that you have the skill sets they need to get their job done. Don't be afraid to invest in this important aspect of making yourself a valuable and marketable asset to any company.

Security Clearances

Some important information you will need to know about getting your paperwork done right is security clearances.

Security clearances are very common in DoD contracting. They are a way to control who has access to what information. A lot of times there is a need for security clearances based on the type of environment you are working in, the type of information you have access to, and the facility that you are entering. I highly recommend that if you don't have a clearance, then get one. A lot of times employers try to pay less on your labor rate due to the expense of getting a clearance. I assure you that the company will make that money back, even if they are footing the bill. A lot of times the government will get the clearance for the company because they want to fill a hard-to-fill spot. The process is pretty simple, and I will touch on each of the main levels, secret, top secret, and poly.

Secret: A lot of times this consists of phone calls, record checks, and assurances you are not on any lists. The amount of time needed from the time you complete your paperwork to the time your clearance is cleared is about six months. It is very quick and mostly done via phone or desktop for the investigator getting you your clearance.

Top secret: This requires a little more effort. There will be phone calls and records checks just like in secret clearance, but there will also be a visit from the investigator to your neighbors and family to check on the information that you gave them. This process can take about a year and is a lot more detailed than the process for a secret clearance. This will also include a sit down with the investigator to discuss such things as why you might have gone out of the country one time, or why did you put down a speeding ticket for offenses that was cleared up? This whole process could take thirty minutes to a couple hours, depending on your lifestyle. I find that the more straight to the point and the more consistent your answers are, the better.

Poly: Depending on the type of poly and how you answer the questions, this should take less than thirty minutes, but it depends on the type of access or the facility you're trying to get cleared for. They could ask anything from "Have you stolen anything over $100?" to "Have you ever kissed your sister?" It just depends on what they are trying to accomplish.

The important thing to remember is that you should answer the questions truthfully. It is not the government's intention to fail you. They just want to determine whether you can handle the responsibility given to you if they allow you access. If you smoked marijuana as a kid and they ask you that question, then answer truthfully. Most questions nowadays are time limited: "Have you done drugs in the last ten years?" "Did you have a court appearance within the last seven years?"

To learn more about clearances and the clearance process I recommend going to the source:

http://www.opm.gov/Forms/pdf_fill/sf85p.pdf

This site explains a bit about the process for clearances. Another one is http://www.opm.gov. This is the government agency that handles the security portion of your clearance.

Remember that each government agency has its own process. The Department of Energy has a different type of clearance than the National Security Agency. I recommend you read up on the particular agency you will be working for in detail.

Chapter 8: Documentation, Documentation, Documentation

While we're on the subject of the paper chase, let's talk a little bit about the importance of documentation to your success. Real estate people have their saying: "Location, location, location!" as being of major importance to the success of their work. For the DoD contractor, a variation of this is appropriate: "Documentation, documentation, documentation!"

Documentation is so important, but it is such an overlooked aspect of the technical field. Documentation is important for different reasons, but documentation will provide a powerful tool for your development and professional growth. A little bit of effort to document in the beginning will assure you have all the information you need for down the road.

I personally have seen topics brought up six months after a project was finished, and no one had a clue as to what went on during the reasonably fresh project, all due to poor documentation standards.

I will say this over and over: if there is no documentation

standard for your job, create one. Just do it, and you will see the benefit as you progress in your career field.

Many IT contractors are hired to troubleshoot a problem. Troubleshooting is basically starting with a problem and then working your way from the closest point to that problem out, till you find the point that is the actual cause. It is really that simple, and you don't need to know verbatim how every piece of equipment works, though having a little knowledge on the device or situation will carry you a long way. Documentation will help you and anyone who goes after you to figure out the shortest route to the problem's solution.

Work Completed

Probably one of the most overlooked aspects of a FSR's job is documenting work that was done on the project that they were hired to work on. It is imperative that good documentation be kept in the form of a journal or log to show what was accomplished and how it was accomplished. In review on future jobs or with some down time, you should be able to glean from the journal some troubleshooting tips, and if you notes are good enough, you would then be able to write white papers or training material for future FSRs. Both of these add to your value as a professional in your field. You can also always prove exactly how much value you added to an operation because you traced your steps.

When I keep a journal, I keep it by the day of the month and also the hours that I was on the job. For example:

12 July 2004

1300L: Completed troubleshooting of USC-60 LNA using a spectrum analyzer that was borrowed from another military unit. After setting up the equipment, began basic honing of the signal to assure that a positive reading was maintained. By doing this I was able to determine that the LNA was not at fault and that there was a loose cable that got bent. Since there is no direct access to the system, by looking at the equipment, I was able to determine that the problem was caused by wear and tear and definitely from the heat and wind. Once this was accomplished, the system was brought back on line and it was maintained and ran for 48 hours with no problems.

1400L: Helped install the Cisco Call Manager with other military personnel. The call manager went in with no problem and the gateway was established and tested prior to the system being brought on line fully.

These are just a couple examples on what should be included and the amount of detail needed, especially if you were assisting the head of the project or heading up the particular project yourself. Remember that you want to put in as much detail as possible so that if the same problem was ever to come up again, you would have the steps and the outcome handy from what you did before.

Often times various pieces of software come with a notes section or something that allows you to post what was done to the system. This is really important with multi-man troubleshooting, and also for shifts, so that they know what was done during the last shift. Generally, it just makes working on a system real easy if the people working on it document what was done and they document it well so that anyone can come up and continue working on the system.

Every now and again you will get a person who feels there is no need to keep good notes because he or she will remember what is going on off the top of the head. I have to sigh at these kinds of people, because no one, no one, can remember all this stuff and remember it as accurately as a good set of notes. The only time that this might be true is if that person worked on only one piece of equipment and nothing else. As a contractor, this is rarely the case.

There will be times when companies really don't have a documentation standard. Then it is up to the individual contractor to really set the standard. Trust me when I say you will save a lot of time and effort down the road if you keep proper notes from the start. Keeping a good WAR (Weekly Activity Report) will also assist you in future work and assure that there is a process and procedure for someone new to follow. Most of the time the WAR is kept as a show of what was accomplished during the week.

Documentation can only help, not hurt, you. It shows you were on the job, doing the job, figuring out the job, and keeping track of the job. It impresses others and helps them. It helps you do that all-important part of being a success: a good job.

Chapter 9: Dealing with the IRS

To do your taxes for work on foreign earned income, you'll want to know all about IRS Form 673.

This is a "Statement for claiming exemption from withholding on foreign earned income eligible for the exclusion(s) provided by Section 911. The following statement, when completed and furnished by a citizen of the United States to his or her employer, permits the employer to exclude from income tax withholding all or a part of the wages paid for services performed outside the United States." (See: http://www.irs.gov/pub/irs-pdf/f673.pdf

Of course, I will start this chapter out with the usual disclaimer: check with your accountant or tax preparer to be sure about this. However, I have used this form for the many years I have been involved in defense contracting. My thinking is that I would prefer that my bank account earn the interest instead of the IRS's bank accounts.

This form takes two minutes to fill out and will assure that no federal taxes are taken from your paycheck as long as you are outside the country. The usual amount of time outside the country to get the full $90,000+ dollars tax break, is 330 days, and normally it's prorated down from there. I don't have the formula handy, but you do not have to be out of country the full 330 days to get some benefit from this filing. Here is the current web URL for this document:

http://www.irs.gov/pub/irs-pdf/f673.pdf

You can also get to it by going to <u>www.irs.gov</u> and typing in the keyword "Form 673" to assure that you have the latest year. This is a very handy form to know about as you plan your financial future through DoD contracting.

Chapter 10: My Firm: Total Technical Solutions

You can find my firm at www.Totaltech.us.com.

What is Total Technical Solutions, LLC? Total Technical Solutions, LLC is a SDVOB Minority owned and operated business. We are registered in Florida State as well as FEDBIZ and CCR for ease of doing business.

Total Technical Solutions, LLC offers solutions to keep IT training and certification costs down without sacrificing quality. No matter what type of individual or business you are, we understand you are doing that because it is what you are good at. That is what makes you successful.

Unfortunately for many individuals and business owners, in order to stay ahead of the competition, you have to stay abreast of today's technologies, which can become a full time job in itself. With Total Technical Solutions, LLC, we help unburden you or your company of the pressure to keep up with and manage today's technologies. Our focal points are the following key competencies:

- Network and Systems design, solutions, support and management
-IT Training and training development

All too often an IT provider simply fixes a problem without any view of the big picture. At Total Technical Solutions, LLC, our primary focus is on the long-term reliability of the IT network and IT staff. Since every client has different priorities, a flexible approach towards information technology is necessary in order to provide viable solutions.

Meeting with the client's key decision makers, we will provide information about real-world solutions currently in use in many different industries. This allows the client to make informed and well-researched decisions. We bring to bear experience and understanding to allow a business's technology to bring as much ROI as possible with the right experience and the right people to achieve success.

`For individuals, we offer offers classes on Network Plus and Security Plus as well as many others.

Check out our website. We are hiring veterans and non-veterans alike to fill various technical and support roles. Please check www.totaltech.us.com for the latest listings and training offerings.

Conclusion

I hope this manual has given you some great ideas about how to launch and maintain a career in the lucrative and satisfying world of Department of Defense contract work. I've tried to show how beneficial it has been for me, and how available it is to many people who never thought of this as a way of life and a way to build a strong and secure financial picture and future for themselves and/or their families.

I hope I have succeeded in giving you some new and useful ideas for your future of success in this always-hiring field. The best of luck to you!